D1480732

First Facts™

Science Tools

Compasses

by Adele Richardson

Consultant:
Dr. Ronald Browne
Associate Professor of Elementary Education
Minnesota State University, Mankato

Capstone *press*

Mankato, Minnesota

First Facts is published by Capstone Press,
151 Good Counsel Drive, P.O. Box 669, Mankato, Minnesota 56002.
www.capstonepress.com

Library of Congress Cataloging-in-Publication Data
Richardson, Adele, 1966–
    Compasses / by Adele Richardson.
        p. cm.—(First facts. Science tools)
    Summary: Introduces the function, parts, and uses of compasses, and provides
instructions for two activities that demonstrate how a compass works.
    Includes bibliographical references and index.
    ISBN 0-7368-2520-7 (hardcover)
    ISBN 0-7368-4957-2 (paperback)
    1. Compass—Juvenile literature. [1. Compass.] I. Title. II. Series.
QC849.R53 2004
912′.0284—dc22   2003013363

Editorial Credits
Christopher Harbo, editor; Juliette Peters, designer; Erin Scott/SARIN Creative, illustrator;
    Deirdre Barton, photo researcher; Eric Kudalis, product planning editor

Photo Credits
Capstone Press/Gary Sundermeyer, 1, 4, 5, 6, 7, 8–9, 12, 13, 16, 17, 18
Capstone Press/GEM Photo Studio/Dan Delaney, cover
Capstone Press/S. Sinnard, 20
Corbis/Layne Kennedy, 14; Phil Schermeister, 15

1 2 3 4 5 6 09 08 07 06 05 04

Table of Contents

The Class Investigates

Mr. Ali's students are using a compass to find **directions**. They find north, south, west, and east. They hang the directions around the classroom.

One student puts a sheet over his head. He looks at his compass. He needs to find east without looking at the directions on the walls.

Turn to page 19 to try this activity!

What Is a Compass?

A compass helps people find direction. The needle inside a compass always points north. It points north no matter how the compass is turned.

A person who finds north can also
find south, west, and east. This student
uses a compass to turn toward the south.

🔍 **Fun Fact:**
A compass should always be held level
so the needle can spin around easily.

Parts of a Compass

A compass has a needle, a **pivot**, and a card. The needle is made of metal. It spins on the pivot. A card is under the needle. It has north, south, east, and west printed on it.

Fun Fact:
Clubs like the Boy Scouts and the Girl Scouts teach their members how to use compasses.

needle

pivot

card

Earth's Magnetic Field

Earth is a huge **magnet**. It has a **magnetic field** that **attracts** some metals. Earth's magnetic field is strongest at its **magnetic poles**. The metal compass needle is attracted to the magnetic north pole.

 Fun Fact:
Magnetic north is not the same as the true north pole. Magnetic north is several hundred miles (kilometers) south of true north.

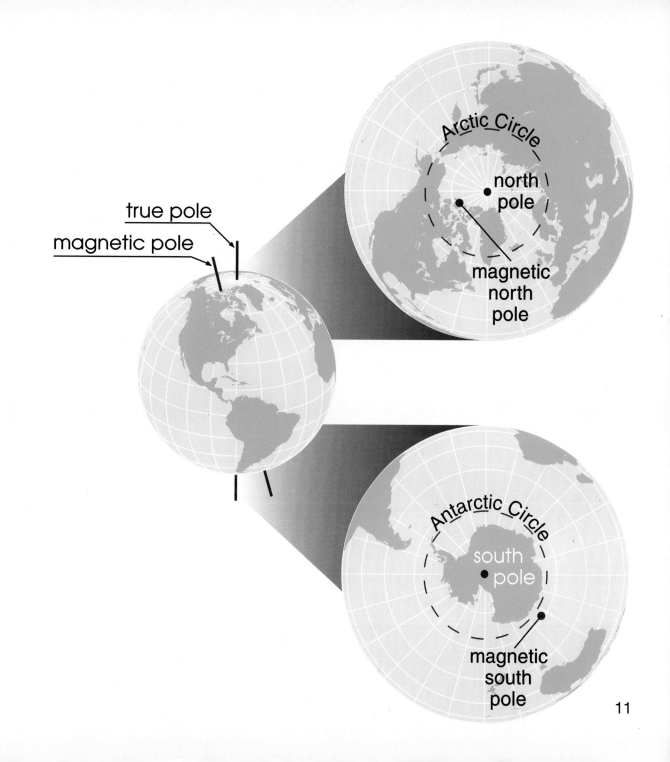

true pole

magnetic pole

Arctic Circle

north
pole

magnetic
north
pole

Antarctic Circle

south
pole

magnetic
south
pole

Compasses in School

Students use compasses to find directions. This class is learning how to find west with a compass.

The students hold their compasses so the W is at the top. Then, they turn their bodies until the needle points to the N. The students are now facing west.

Other Uses for Compasses

Compasses are used on boats and airplanes. Ship captains and pilots use compasses to travel in the right direction.

Hikers use compasses in the wilderness. If lost, hikers may use compasses to find their way to safety.

 Fun Fact:
Some compasses come with wristbands. They can be worn like watches.

Hundreds of years ago, people made compasses with cork and pieces of iron. You can make a compass with materials found around your house.

Try It!

What You Need

small bowl
water
small nail
magnet
plastic milk cap
compass

What You Do

1. Fill the bowl with water.
2. Rub the nail from the head to the point with the magnet. Each stroke must go in the same direction. The nail should be rubbed 40 to 50 times.
3. Lay the nail on the plastic milk cap. Carefully set the cap in the bowl of water.

The cap will spin a little in the bowl. When it stops, the nail should point north. Use a compass to make sure it points north.

What Did They Learn?

Mr. Ali's students tried to find directions with a compass. See if you can use a compass to find north, south, west, and east.

Try It!

What You Need

marker

4 sheets of paper

compass

tape

light-colored bed sheet

a friend

What You Do

1. Write the letters N, S, W, and E each on separate sheets of paper.
2. Place your compass on the floor in the middle of the room. Rotate the compass so that the needle is pointing at the N on the compass card.
3. Tape the piece of paper with the letter N on the wall the compass needle points toward.
4. Tape the other pieces of paper on the south, west, and east walls.
5. Pick up the compass and stand in the center of the room.
6. Cover your head with a light-colored bed sheet. Make sure you can still read the compass underneath the sheet.
7. Slowly turn yourself around several times.
8. Ask your friend to call out north, south, east, or west.
9. Under the sheet, use your compass to find the direction named. When you think you are facing the right direction, take off the sheet. See if you found the correct direction.

People use compasses and horses in a sport called Competitive Mounted Orienteering (CMO). In CMO, people ride horses through courses set up in forests and other outdoor areas. CMO riders use compasses with maps to find checkpoints on the course.

What Do You Think?

1. On a compass, northwest is the middle point between north and west. Where would southeast be? Try to find northwest and southeast with a compass.

2. Compasses are used on boats and airplanes. Where else have you seen compasses being used?

3. Compasses always point north. How would you know what direction is south by using a compass? How would you find east and west?

4. A compass works because its needle is drawn to Earth's magnetic north pole. What would happen if the needle was made of plastic instead of metal?

Glossary

attract (uh-TRAKT)—when two objects pull together; a magnet attracts iron.

direction (duh-REK-shuhn)—the way something or someone is moving; north, south, west, and east are directions.

magnet (MAG-nit)—a piece of metal that attracts iron or steel

magnetic field (mag-NET-ik FEELD)—the area around a magnet that has the power to attract magnetic metals

magnetic pole (mag-NET-ik POHL)—either of the two regions near the north and south pole toward which a compass needle points

pivot (PIV-uht)—a point on which something else turns or balances

Read More

Sharth, Sharon. *Way to Go!: Finding Your Way with a Compass.* Reader's Digest Explorer Guides. Pleasantville, NY: Reader's Digest, 2000.

Trumbauer, Lisa. *You Can Use a Compass.* Rookie Read-About Science. New York: Children's Press, 2003.

Internet Sites

FactHound offers a safe, fun way to find Internet sites related to this book. All of the sites on FactHound have been researched by our staff.

Here's how:
1. Visit *www.facthound.com*
2. Type in this special code **0736825207** for age-appropriate sites. Or enter a search word related to this book for a more general search.
3. Click on the **Fetch It** button.

FactHound will fetch the best sites for you!

Index